# ANIMAL
# [Penguin]
# DIARIES

STEVE PARKER

QEB

Copyright © QEB Publishing 2014

First published in the United States in 2014 by
QEB Publishing, Inc.
3 Wrigley, Suite A
Irvine, CA 92618
www.qed-publishing.co.uk

A CIP record for this book is available from the Library of Congress.

ISBN 978 1 60992 502 4

**Project Editor** Carey Scott
**Illustrator** Peter David Scott/The Art Agency
**Designer** Dave Ball
**Editorial Assistant** Tasha Percy
**Managing Editor** Victoria Garrard
**Design Manager** Anna Lubecka

Printed and bound in China

Photo Credits
Key: t = top, b = bottom, c = center,
**Alamy** 18b All Canada Photos; **Corbis** 18c Frans Lanting; **Getty** 7 Ben Cranke/
The Image Bank, 16 Doug Allen/The Image Bank; **Shutterstock** 18t DenisNata;
Gordan, and David M. Scrader, Luminis, Oleg Golovnev, Ana de Sousa, Valentin
Agapov, Dementeva, Petr Jilek all background images.

# Contents

Me strutting my stuff!

Feeding Time ... 4

Lucky Escape! ... 6

The Great March ... 8

Pairing Up ... 10

Egg Exchange ... 12

A Long Winter ... 14

Hello Chick! ... 16

Family Life ... 18

Back to the Sea ... 20

Ocean Friends ... 22

Killers! ... 24

Taking Turns ... 26

Farewell to the Ice ... 28

What They Say About Me ... 30

Tricky Terms ... 31

Index ... 32

# Feeding Time

Zoom, swoosh, whoosh—it's food time! I'm going to swish after a fish, just like I did with that squid, then I'll grab a crab or kill some krill! I love swimming, diving, and feasting in the Great Ocean during the warm summer. It makes up for those boring winter months standing on the ice with an egg on my feet.

When I was little I learned how to swim, dive, and feed from my instruction book, *Becoming Perfect Penguins*. I'm an expert now. Today I caught and gulped down five silverfish in one dive!

## SWIMMING AND DIVING
### Basic flipper-flap

A penguin's wings, or flippers, are designed to swim. However, you still flap them up and down, like a flying bird. A slight twist of the wrist makes the flipper tilt with each stroke to push water backward—and you forward.

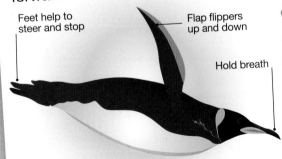

Feet help to steer and stop

Flap flippers up and down

Hold breath

## PENGUIN POSTURE

As a beginner, it is best to keep your body straight, or you will simply go around in circles!

We swim with our flipper-wings.

Plenty of fish in the sea!

There's no escape from my sharp beak.

# Emperor Penguin

**Group** Birds—penguins

**Adult length** 4 feet

**Weight** Up to 110 pounds

**Habitat** Ice and oceans around Antarctica.

**Food** Fish, squid, krill, and similar sea creatures.

**Features** Flippers, sharp beak, good eyesight, thick feathers, and layer of fat under skin to keep in body warmth.

My favorite trick is to hold my breath, dive deep, and look up to spot prey just below the ocean surface or under an ice ~~flow~~ floe. I race up fast, grab one, swallow it, swim back down, and then do it all over again.

# Lucky Escape!

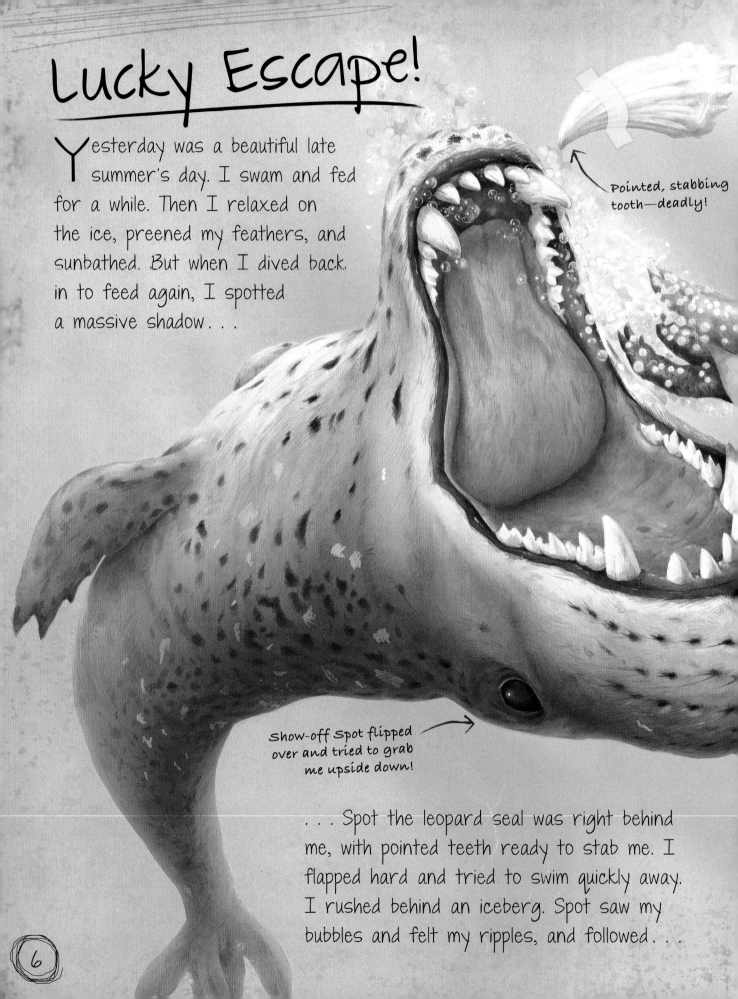

Yesterday was a beautiful late summer's day. I swam and fed for a while. Then I relaxed on the ice, preened my feathers, and sunbathed. But when I dived back in to feed again, I spotted a massive shadow...

Pointed, stabbing tooth—deadly!

Show-off Spot flipped over and tried to grab me upside down!

... Spot the leopard seal was right behind me, with pointed teeth ready to stab me. I flapped hard and tried to swim quickly away. I rushed behind an iceberg. Spot saw my bubbles and felt my ripples, and followed...

This poor penguin was slower than me!

Seals have a crushing bite.

# Leopard Seal

**Group** Mammals—seals and sea lions

**Adult length** 12 feet

**Weight** Up to 1,320 pounds

**Habitat** Ice and oceans around Antarctica.

**Food** Penguins and other seabirds, fish, krill, squid, smaller seals.

**Features** Flippers, pointed teeth, thick fur with spots, layer of fat under skin to keep body warm.

I can't look around—too scary!

Keep head straight for fast-forward.

. . .So I dived down deep, then swam straight up at top speed to leap above the surface and land on the iceberg. That's the nearest penguins get to flying. Safe at last!

# The Great March

**I**n the summer, it was light at night too. We feasted, and our bodies stored the extra food for energy during the long winter to come. But now it's fall and getting dark—time to leave the Great Ocean for our long trek across the ice.

## South Polar Skua

**Group** Birds—skuas, gulls, and waders

**Adult length** 1.8 feet

**Weight** Up to 3 pounds

**Habitat** Oceans and coasts around Antarctica in summer, other oceans in winter.

**Food** Fish, eggs, and chicks of penguins and other seabirds.

**Features** Hooked beak, powerful wings, broad tail. Attacks other birds to make them drop their food.

Good-bye Great Ocean!

Toboggan across Frozen Flat.

### DANGERS ON THE WAY

1. Crevasses—deep cracks in the ice.
2. Icefalls—caused by melting.
3. Heatstroke—from too much sun.

Every few hours I pause to rest.

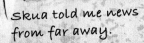

Skua told me news from far away.

On the way I met Skua. She sometimes ~~mygreats~~ migrates or flies away to a warmer place for midwinter. Skua says breeding here on the ice, like we do, is crazy. But she'll be back later—to try and steal our chicks!

We slide past Frozen Blocks.

Waddling down White Hill is slippery.

The climb up Big Glacier is really tiring.

At last we reach The Rookery.

It takes many days to reach The Rookery, where we gather to breed. I learned the way by following the others. But I'm still not sure why we march quite so far. Skua says it's more than 60 miles! Maybe it's to escape from enemies like Spot and Keira the killer whale.

# Pairing Up

I looked for My Partner from last year. I hope she has survived the summer and returned. But it's unlikely—only about one penguin pair in seven get together again the following year.

Everyone looks for a partner.

I greet my partner and we touch beaks!

I spread my flippers, looked up and called: "Caa-ca-ca-caah!" It's my "ecstatic pose" that no female can resist. I heard an answer from My Partner! We touched beaks to say hello.

## COURTSHIP RITUALS

1. Male calls in ecstatic pose.

2. Male and female greet and slowly raise beaks.

3. Female follows male as he waddles around the colony.

4. Both bow and rub beaks before mating.

Watching the new creature.

Five legs, three eyes— very odd!

Partners waddle around together.

We waddled, bowed, and stretched to show each other we were healthy, well fed, and able to be good parents. It's called ~~kortchip~~ ~~kortship~~ courtship. A strange new big-eyed creature watched us, but it caused no trouble, so we ignored it.

# Egg Exchange

It's been more than a month since we arrived at The Rookery. It's nearly midwinter and the sun hardly rises. Now for the tricky part. My Partner lays our egg—then I take over.

We prepare to swap the egg.

## OUR EGG

Length: 5 inches

Width: 3 inches

Weight: 1 pound

Color: Pale greeny white

Lifesize Emperor Penguin egg.

My Partner quickly gathers the egg onto her feet. Then we waddle close together and she nudges and edges the egg onto my feet. Slowly, carefully, so it cannot fall . . . success!

She passes the precious egg to me.

It's time for My Partner to leave. Making the egg has used up all her energy, and she's tired and hungry. She sets off for the Great Ocean. I'm stuck here with all the other males and our eggs. Oh well. Snowy has come to say hello.

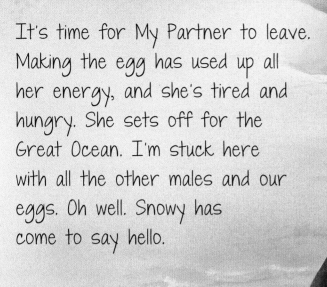

Snowy passes through.

Good-bye, My Partner!

I settle the egg on my feet.

## Snow Petrel

**Group** Birds—petrels, shearwaters, and albatrosses

**Adult length** 1.3 feet

**Weight** 12 ounces

**Habitat** Oceans, coasts, and islands around Antarctica.

**Food** Krill, fish, squid, carcasses.

**Features** Pure white feathers, black eyes and beak, gray-blue feet. Flies farther south than any other bird.

# A Long Winter

I count the days from when My Partner leaves to when our chick hatches. Last year it was 65! I'm on Day 17 today. It's quite chilly already, as shown by this cold-o-meter left by one of the new creatures.

°F °C

My inner body.

My hottest day ever!

Liquid water freezes into solid ice.

Average spring day.

Today's reading.

100

80

60

40

20

0

-20

-40

40

30

20

10

0

-10

-20

-30

-40

Day 24: Similar to Day 23. Day 31: I stood in the middle of the huddle for a long time. It was so hot! Days 34-38: A tremendous blizzard blew, brrr. Day 41: I'm getting bored now. Day 42: I'm also very hungry . . .

## KEEPING WARM
## Fat and feathers
You must clean and preen your two layers of feathers using your beak and foot claws. The outer feathers are strong, windproof, and waterproof. The inner ones, called down, are soft and fluffy. They, and your under-skin fat, keep in your body warmth.

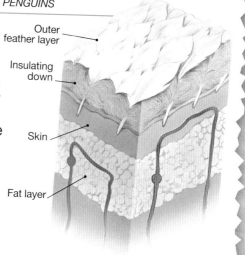

Outer feather layer

Insulating down

Skin

Fat layer

Bad luck— my turn to be extra-cold on the outside today!

## WHAT I DO IN THE HUDDLE

1. Take turns on the outside.

2. Keep my back to the wind.

3. My egg stays on my feet.

4. No pushing!

# Hello Chick!

Day 56: It's gradually getting lighter during the day and warmer at night. Day 61: Similar to Day 60. Day 62: I thought I felt the egg move slightly. Day 63: Yes, there's tapping and pecking inside. This is so exciting!

The Rookery is now busy and noisy.

Chick feeds on my "gullet milk."

Day 64: Hello Chick! It took two days for her to peck through the tough shell. Now Chick is warm on my feet, under my fold of skin, fat, and feathers. I feed Chick a thick milk I make inside my own food tube, my ~~gilut~~ gullet.

Our beaks are a great weapon.

I fight off Pesky Petrel . . .

. . .but other petrels get lucky.

## Southern Giant Petrel

**Group** Birds—petrels, shearwaters, and albatrosses

**Adult length** 3.3 feet

**Weight** Up to 17.5 pounds

**Habitat** Southern oceans, coasts, and islands.

**Food** Krill, squid, fish, eggs and chicks of seabirds, carcasses.

**Features** Large hooked beak, powerful wings 6.5 feet across. Vomits at enemies.

Pesky Petrel is a big strong bird who swoops down and tries to steal our chicks. I peck back hard, squawk, and wave my flippers. If I leave Chick for just a second or two, all my hard work and care will be wasted.

# Family Life

At last! The females are here after their two-month trip. They trekked to the Great Ocean, fed well, and came all the way back. Among them is My Partner. What a relief, or I'd be stuck with Chick! What a relief, or I'd be stuck with Chick!

Females return to The Rookery.

My Partner will take over Chick care now.

White Duck's chick is so fluffy!

Here's my chick—THE CHICK!

Petrel's chick is not so cute.

Check out some of the other chicks that live around here. We all have fluffy feathers to protect us from the cold, but some chicks are cuter than others!

Hungry males set off for the sea.

We bow, touch beaks, and call out greetings. It's the first time Chick has seen her mother. Mother has masses of smelly fishy food in her belly. She will ~~regerjitate~~ regurgitate or "cough up" some for Chick.

A female looks after an unhatched egg.

I'm ready to leave. Bye Chick!

Some eggs never hatch. Tragic.

Now it's my turn to leave. I'm starving—I haven't eaten for almost four months! I'll march back to the Great Ocean with all the other hungry males. Left-right, left-right, slide for a while, left-right. . .

# Back to the Sea

Here we are, back at the Great Ocean. Before diving in, a quick check for Spot and Keira. All clear. Even so, I hang back, just in case they're nearby. The first penguins in are the ones most likely to get eaten.

I love fish. Lanternfish are double-amazing—they glow in the dark and they taste terrific! Skua, who likes measuring things, says they are 6 inches long.

Skua says the longest I've held my breath is 18 minutes . . .

Skua says my fastest swim is 20 feet per second.

Krill are small but juicy.

Southern lanternfish have spiky fins.

Krill look like shrimp or prawns, and a big shoal has millions! But their outsides are quite crunchy. Also they are smaller than my beak. So I have to eat a hundred or more each day to feel full.

My deepest dive is 1,730 feet.

## WATCHING MY WEIGHT

Each summer I eat well and get heavy. During the winter egg-caring I can't eat. Although I sleep 20 hours a day to save energy, I still lose almost half my body weight each winter.

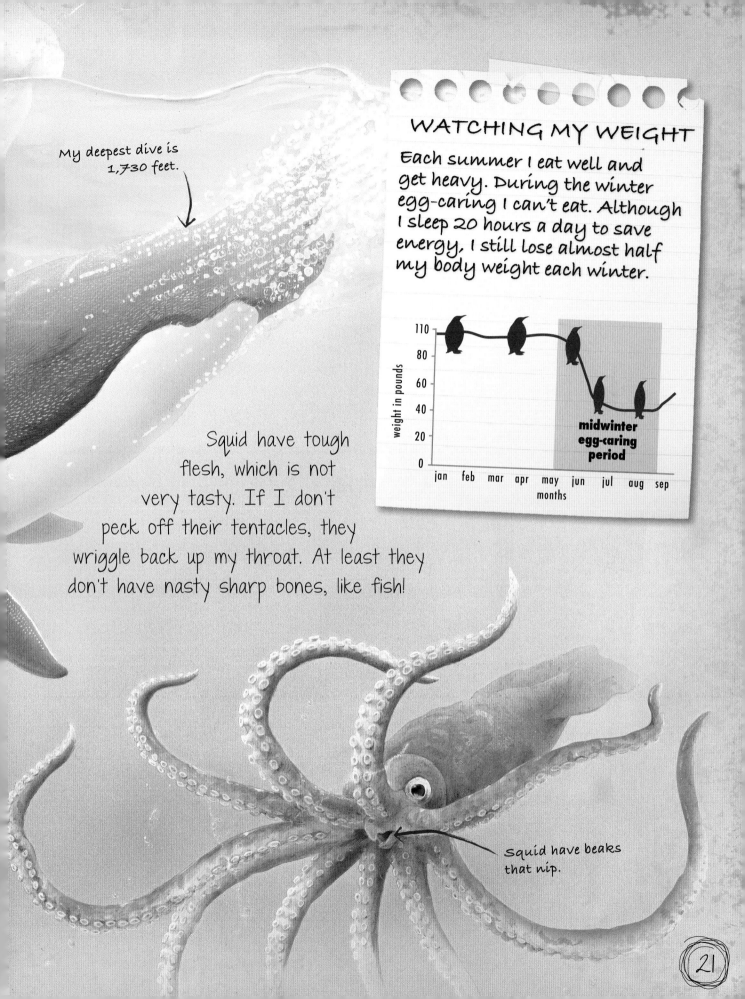

weight in pounds

110
80
60
40
20
0

jan feb mar apr may jun jul aug sep

months

**midwinter egg-caring period**

Squid have tough flesh, which is not very tasty. If I don't peck off their tentacles, they wriggle back up my throat. At least they don't have nasty sharp bones, like fish!

Squid have beaks that nip.

# Ocean Friends

I've been feeding well for the last week, and I feel much better. Today I chatted with some of my friends in the Great Ocean. We talked about waves and currents, where the shoals of fish and krill are, and if there are any dangers in the area.

Long whiskers feel for food.

Weddy is friendly. . . for a seal. She eats similar food to me, like fish, krill, and squid. But I am careful because, if she was starving, she might snack on a penguin.

## Weddell Seal

**Group** Mammals—seals and sea lions

**Adult length** 10 feet

**Weight** 1,100 pounds

**Habitat** Oceans and shores around Antarctica.

**Food** Krill, fish, squid, penguins, and other seabirds.

**Features** Flipper-shaped limbs, big eyes, thick fur and fat under skin to keep in body warmth.

Gills help fish breathe underwater (which I can't).

Spike the Antarctic toothfish is one of the biggest fish around here. She eats all kinds of food, and even bites parts off of dead whales! Yuck!

## WHO DIVES DEEPEST?

In a diving contest, Weddy and I would lose. Spike wins longest dive. Being a fish, she never surfaces for air!

Rear flippers for steering and speed-bursts.

depth in feet

| | |
|---|---|
| 0 | |
| 1,500 | Weddell Seal 1,150 feet |
| | Me 1,700 feet |
| 3,000 | |
| 5,000 | Antarctic Toothfish 6,500 feet |
| 6,500 | |
| | Southern Elephant Seal More than 7,500 feet |
| 8,000 | |

Elly is an Elephant Seal.

Elly says he's the world's biggest seal—over 8,800 pounds, and 20 feet long! He roars by blowing through his long, floppy nose, which he says is like an elephant's trunk.

Elly holds his breath for two hours—gasp!

# Killers!

**W**e were feeding on a big shoal of fish, then suddenly about six killer whales surrounded us. They are so big, strong, and smart. I know the chief of the group, Keira. She's really sneaky and organizes their hunting.

Keira "spyhopped"—she rose up out of the water to look at the scene.

Look out—near the edge is most dangerous.

All of us penguins swam fast to leap out of the water onto an ice floe. We all made it, but the floe was crowded. The killers circled, waiting for one of us to fall in.

Another floe of frightened penguins ~~floeted~~ floated by. Keira swam around it, then poked up her head and spied that the floe was very small. She told the other killers to bump and tilt the floe, until some of the penguins fell in. What a terrible fate!

These poor penguins can't escape!

Killers tipping over the small floe. Cunning!

I stayed well away from the edge.

## Killer Whale

**Group** Mammals—whales and dolphins

**Adult length** Male 30 feet, female 23 feet

**Weight** Up to 16,000 pounds

**Habitat** All the world's seas and oceans.

**Food** Fish, seals and sea lions, seabirds, whales, squid, and penguins!

**Features** Black and white markings, two-lobed tail, tall back fin. Very clever, they work together to hunt prey.

# Taking Turns

Full to bursting after my fantastic feast, I return to Chick. Some of the youngsters are big and strong, but still with fluffy baby feathers. Parents take turns, one staying with the chick while the other goes to feed at sea.

Hungry parents head to the sea.

Full males and females return.

Parents find their chicks by calling.

Skua is back, and hungry!

## Antarctic Prion

**Group** Birds—petrels, shearwaters, and albatrosses

**Adult length** 1 foot

**Weight** 4–7 ounces

**Habitat** All southern oceans, coasts, and islands.

**Food** Krill, shrimp, worms, plankton, tiny sea creatures, and plants.

**Features** White eyebrow, blue feet, brown back, saw-edged beak to filter tiny food from sea water.

Another bird friend, Pri, is here to breed. She reckons it's more sensible to raise chicks in summer, when the sea is full of food, rather than in winter like we do. Too true!

Pri tells me the news.

It's early summer, much warmer, and the ice edge is melting back. Each journey between the Great Ocean and The Rookery is shorter than the last one. The Rookery is busier than ever.

Partners bow and coo when reunited.

Parent feeds chick.

This crèche will get bigger, so animals won't attack.

My Partner and I will make about five feeding trips each. Then, when Chick is a bit older, she will stay safe and warm in a group called a ~~kresh~~ crèche while we both look for food.

# Farewell to the Ice

Some chicks lost their baby feathers and now have their strong, waterproof adult plumage. It's midsummer, the sun never sets, and we've all left The Rookery. So much ice has melted, the march to the Great Ocean seems to get shorter every year.

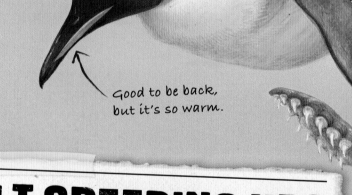

I chatted with my friend Adélie, a smaller type of penguin, about how the water feels warmer each year. She agreed that it's not good. Penguins overheat easily!

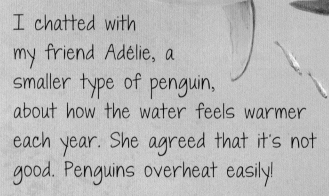

Good to be back, but it's so warm.

## IS THE BIG MELT SPEEDING UP?

*Aerial view of melting ice taken by our flying reporter Albert Ross*

Every year, Antarctic residents make more complaints about less ice, warmer water, and reduced food. Whales moan that krill is scarce. Seals and penguins argue over fewer fish. Squid suffer sucker-rot. Killer whales get heatstroke. A spokespenguin said: "It's worse every year. We blame Net-Boats. They are noisy, churn up the sea, and spew out horrible oil. If you get too near, you can feel their heat. Their nets steal our food—and can drown you."

Our chick has just a few baby feathers.

Adélie wonders why it's warmer.

The older chicks now look like adults.

Beware Colossus' long grabbers!

Back at sea, Colossus lurks below. She also says it's warmer, and food is less common. Now don't get me wrong, I love being a penguin—but if my flippers were proper wings, I'd fly far, far away . . .

## Colossal Squid

**Group** Mollusks—shellfish, snails, octopus, and squid

**Adult length** 40 feet

**Weight** 1,100 pounds

**Habitat** Southern oceans.

**Food** Fish, other squid, octopus, arrow-worms, penguins.

**Features** Two long grabbing tentacles and eight shorter ones, hooks and suckers on tentacles, rear fin.

# What They Say About Me

My diary describes what I think of all the creatures I meet. But what do they think of me? Let's find out. . .

> " I love emperor penguins! If I catch one leaving the sea for its Rookery, it makes a two-course meal—bird outside, fish inside! "

Killer Whale

Prion

> " Penguins can't fly, so I bring them the news from far away. And, unlike their so-called friend Skua, I won't try to steal their chicks. But penguins' winter breeding is just crazy! "

> " We had a breath-holding contest once. Penguin did 18 minutes—excellent for an emperor. But I won of course. I didn't breathe out for over an hour, then I got bored and gave up. "

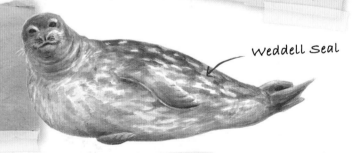

Weddell Seal

Snow Petrel

> " Hi. It's cool that penguins are slow and dim-witted—I don't have to stress to catch one. I just cruise around, chill, and watch and wait for my moment. Then—BITE! "

> " Penguins are sooo last year. I'm sooo the boss! I eat their eggs and chicks, and steal food from them or other seabirds. So they call me Pesky Petrel. "

Leopard Seal

# Tricky Terms

**Blizzard** A storm in very cold conditions, with heavy snowfall and strong winds.

**Courtship** A display by an animal to show willingness to mate with its partner.

**Crèche** A group of young animals cared for by those who are not their parents.

**Crevasse** A deep crack in a large area of ice, such as in a glacier or iceberg.

**Current** Large amount of flowing water, such as in a river, along the seashore, or through the ocean.

**Glacier** A river that is frozen into solid ice and moves downhill very slowly.

**Gullet** The tube for swallowed food, from the mouth and throat down into the stomach.

**Iceberg** A huge floating lump of frozen fresh water, like a chunk that breaks from a glacier's edge and floats in the ocean.

**Icefall** A glacier with lots of cracks, broken melting chunks, and icicles–like a frozen waterfall.

**Ice floe** A floating lump of frozen salty sea water, usually more than 65 feet (20 m) across.

**Krill** Small sea creatures similar to shrimp or prawns, found in all oceans. They are eaten by many sea animals including penguins, seals, and whales.

**Mammal** A warm-blooded animal that has fur or hair, an inner skeleton of bones, and feeds its young on mother's milk.

**Migrate** To go on a long journey to move between places that have the best conditions, such as food and shelter.

**Plumage** The feathers of a bird, including their shapes, colors, and patterns.

**Regurgitate** To bring from the stomach up the gullet (food tube) into the mouth (like humans do when we "throw up"). The opposite of swallowing.

**Rookery** A place where birds, such as penguins, gather to breed each year.

**Shoal** A group of fish or similar water animals that gather near each other in the same area, but swim about in different, random directions.

**Spyhop** When a whale or dolphin holds itself upright and pokes its head and upper body above the surface into the air, usually to look around.

**Tentacles** Long, slim, bendy body parts, used for grabbing, feeding, sensing, and movement, as on a squid or octopus.

> The surface is usually too warm and bright for a deep-sea monster like myself. But when I do swim up, a penguin makes a fluffy mini-feast.

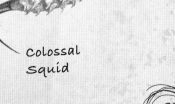

colossal squid

# Index

Adélie penguins 28, 29
Antarctic prions 26, 30
Antarctic toothfish 22, 23

beaks 5, 8, 10, 11, 17, 19, 21, 26
blizzards 15, 31
breath-holding 5, 20, 23, 30
breeding 9, 26

calls 10, 11, 19, 26
chicks 9, 16-17, 18, 19, 26, 27, 28, 29
colossal squid 29, 31
courtship rituals 10, 11, 31
crèches 27, 31
crevasses 8, 31
currents 22, 31

dangers 6-7, 8, 17, 24-25
down 15
ducks 18

ecstatic pose 10, 11
eggs 12-13, 16
emperor penguins 5
eyesight 5

fat 5, 7, 15, 16, 22
feathers 6, 15, 18, 26, 28, 29
filter feeding 26
fishing boats 28
flippers 4, 10, 22
food 4, 8, 16, 19, 20-21, 22

glaciers 9, 31
gullet milk 16

huddles 15
humans 11

icebergs 6, 7, 31
icefalls 8, 31
ice floes 5, 24, 25, 31

killer whales 24-25, 28, 30
krill 20, 22, 28

lanternfish 20
leopard seals 6-7, 30

mammals 7, 22, 25, 31
melting ice 8, 27, 28
migration 8-9, 31

partners 10-11, 12-13, 18, 19, 27
petrels 13, 17, 18, 30
plumage 28, 31
preening 6, 15

regurgitation 19, 31
rookeries 9, 16, 27, 31

seals 6-7, 22, 23, 28, 30
shoals 20, 22, 31
snow petrels 13, 30
South polar skuas 8, 9, 26
southern elephant seals 23
southern giant petrels 17, 18
spyhopping 24, 31
squid 21, 22, 28, 29, 31
swimming and diving 4, 5, 7, 21, 23

temperatures 14
tentacles 21, 29, 31

waddling 9, 11, 12
warm, keeping 5, 15
Weddell seals 22, 23, 30
weight 21